THE COMMON GRIEF

poems by Roberto Sosa

translated by
Jo Anne Engelbert

CURBSTONE PRESS

Printed in the United States on acid-free paper by BookCrafters
Cover design: Stone Graphics
Cover photo by Layle Silbert

Curbstone Press is a 501(c)(3) nonprofit publishing house whose
operations are supported in part by private donations and by
grants from ADCO Foundation, J. Walton Bissell Foundation, Inc.,
Witter Bynner Foundation for Poetry, Inc., Connecticut
Commission on the Arts, Connecticut Arts Endowment Fund,
Lannan Foundation, LEF Foundation, Lila Wallace-Reader's Digest
Literary Publishers Marketing Development Program,
administered by the Council of Literary Magazines and Presses,
The Andrew W. Mellon Foundation, National Endowment for the
Arts Literature, National Endowment for the Arts International
Projects Initiative, and The Plumsock Fund.

Library of Congress Cataloging-in-Publication Data

Sosa, Roberto.
     [Máscara suelta. English & Spanish]
     The common grief / by Roberto Sosa ; translated by Jo Anne
Engelbert.
          p.   cm.
     English and Spanish.
     Contents: The lifted mask — The weeping of things.
     ISBN 1-880684-23-3 : $10.95 (pbk.)
     1. Sosa, Roberto. Translations into English.   I. Engelbert, Jo Anne.   II.
Sosa, Roberto. Llanto de las cosas. English & Spanish. III. Title.
PQ7509.2.S6A22   1994
861—dc20   94-31896

CURBSTONE PRESS
321 Jackson Street, Willimantic, CT 06226

contents

MÁSCARA SUELTA
THE LIFTED MASK

INTRODUCTION

"I would never have imagined that the unprofitable business of weaving verses could endanger my life," Sosa writes in the introduction to his collected works (1990). If books like *Los pobres. Un mundo para todos dividido* and *Secreto militar* won high praise and prestigious literary prizes outside Honduras, within the country they were labeled "antimilitarist" and "highly dangerous." During the height of the "Yankee occupation" that coincided with the Contra war, not only were Sosa's books banned, but he also lost his post at the university and received numerous death threats—certain signs that in Honduras, as in the other countries of Central America, poetry is taken very seriously. When I walk with Sosa through the streets of Tegucigalpa, we have to stop every few steps because people want to greet him, shake his hand, touch his sleeve. "Buenos días, Poeta," they say—"Poeta," as one might say "Maestro," "Doctor" or "Reverendo Padre." For the indigenous peoples of the isthmus, a poet was a seer, a flute played by the gods, a conduit between heaven and earth through which truth might enter the world. If the poetic word is perceived as powerful today, it is because poets like Roberto Sosa have used it to speak the truth.

In Sosa's lifetime there has been much to denounce. Born in Yoro in 1930, Sosa's childhood coincided with the dictatorship of Tiburcio Carías Andino, a period of severe political repression. In "Memorias 1/ 2" he tells us, "my earliest memory starts at a burnt-out streetlight / and ends at a public spigot dripping in a dead alley. / My second memory trickles from a corpse / a procession of corpses violently dead." Among many injustices and horrors Sosa has witnessed, he saw his father ("the kindest human being I have ever known") contract blue lung as a consequence of working as a *venero* or fumigator on a Standard Fruit banana plantation. His mother, the tender and stoic subject of "The Weeping of Things," taught him to read and write, but times were hard, and at the age of five or six, he had to go to work. His job was selling bread on the train that carried the banana workers to the plantation: the beleaguered boy in the poem "The Child" is Sosa himself. Fortunately, he was able to attend school, and in the fifth grade he received his first "book" of poems, a handmade anthology laboriously copied by the rural schoolmaster for his students. Reading that little collection of verses was a critical experience: "I learned that pages of poetry have the power to console," he recalls. Denied a scholarship to attend high school by the dictator's "intellectual bodyguard," Sosa nevertheless managed to continue studying. In 1947 he found a battered copy of a book that was to become a powerful influence in his life: Giovanni Papini's *A Man— Finished*. Reading Papini was the intellectual awakening that would impel him to begin to read voraciously, if chaotically—Nietzsche, Schopenhauer, Goethe, Anatole France, Socrates, Plato, Homer, Dante, Virgil, Bocaccio, Oscar Wilde, Voltaire, Arthur Conan Doyle, Homer, Edgar Allan Poe, Macauley, Knut Hamsun, Kafka ... and to move to the capital to make contact with the intellectual world. He arrived in Tegucigalpa as the Carías repression was ending, made the acquaintance of many writers and began to write poetry. His early books, *Caligramas* (1959), *Muros* (1966) and *Mar interior* (1967), each included a number of arresting poems, but it was not until the publication of two books, *Los pobres* (1969) and *Un mundo para todos dividido* (1971), that Roberto Sosa received international acclaim. *Los pobres* won the Adonaïs Prize in Spain and *Mundo* won the Casa de las Américas Prize in Cuba; within a short time Latin America recognized Sosa as a major poetic talent, to be compared with Vallejo and Neruda for the clarity of his commitment to social justice and for his absolute control of language.

Ironically, just as *Mundo* was being praised throughout the Spanish-speaking world, publication of the book was halted by Honduran authorities. The bloody crises of the seventies in Latin America and the increasingly humiliating role played by Honduras in Central American conflicts triggered a cycle of satirical poems called *Secreto Militar*, published in 1985. The title poem is brief but poignant: "The history of Honduras / could be written on a gun / a shot / a drop of blood." Sosa vents his political ire here in caustic vignettes: portraits of infamous strong men—Somoza, Duvalier, Stroessner, Carías, Franco, Pinochet, Trujillo—and scenes from history, beginning with the Salvadoran massacre of 1932 known as La Matanza. The book served as a necessary exorcism which has enabled Sosa to write today of political themes with a terrible and timeless calm. His pen, tempered by the experience of writing *Secreto militar*, is the more lethal for its subtlety.

The two parts of *The Common Grief*, "The Weeping of Things" and "The Lifted Mask," were originally conceived as separate books and are presented as such in Sosa's collected works. Fruit of the poet's personal and literary maturity, the two cycles of poems, composed simultaneously between 1982 and 1987, constitute a distillation of all he has learned from life and art. Each part represents one of the poles of his poetic creation. Though all the poems are about love, "The Weeping of Things" crystallized around agape—selfless love, his own and others', for the miracles of daily life—and "The Lifted Mask" around eros, a realm little explored in Sosa's previous poetry.

The phrase "the weeping of things"—*lacrimae rerum*—is from the *Aeneid*. Virgil employs it to name the sadness that seems to emanate from things after a massive tragedy; Aeneas contemplates the ravages of battle; Sosa, the suffering and ignominy of his people. If a permanent melancholy is the logical legacy of the Conquest and its aftermath, underlying it is the ancestral melancholy of indigenous Mesoamerica, where long before the arrival of Europeans, poet/philosophers marked the flight of time with poems steeped in sadness. Modern history, particularly events of recent decades, have made sadness the ground of being in much of Central America. Against the darkness of mourning, Sosa sets the small lights of his existence. He calls these poems "elegiac," and indeed many of them honor individuals long dead. Most, however, are "elegies in life" that honor the living; Sosa's mother, now nearing ninety, is lovingly evoked as the intermediary "who read our thoughts, / sensed by their chill the proximity of snakes / and talked to roses—she, the delicate balance / between / human hardness and the weeping of things." All the poems are in some way tributes to indispensable elements of daily life. Some of these are human beings—mother, wife, friends; some are objects—a certain church spire, books, Sosa's old Pontiac; still others are childhood memories—the "widowed insect" that flew above the schoolyard, the little horse asleep in the drawing pad. Brightest of all are the candles lit to the human qualities that make existence endurable—loyalty, courage, commitment to justice. Poems, according to Sosa, meant to "deal a whopping blow to that whore of whores, Death."

Erotic poetry is so rare in Hispanic literature that poets who attempt it must create not only a language but a tradition. In "The Lifted

Mask" Sosa gravitated toward the slow rhythms of longer and longer lines and sensual, dreamlike imagery. Now and then there is a flash of the surreal, like the wild leap of the "hablucinated fish" (el pez azulinante) in "The Station and the Pact." Though intricate and mysterious, the poems were not meant to be obscure. Rather, each is meant to be "a labyrinth of mirrors in which the reader, once the glass door has closed, can wander, out of time."

Most erotic poetry reduces woman to a still life, in Sosa's view, "an exotic fruit reposing on a sheet." Sosa wanted to portray woman as a subject, to use the power of erotic language to reveal a human being who is at once lover, companion and defender of the hearth, the triple personality of "She." If the poems of Weeping portray women as subjects in history—the guerrilla fighter in "On Hate," the women of GAM or the Plaza de Mayo in *The Common Grief*, those of "The Lifted Mask" reveal woman as active subject of the poet's emotional life. Sister in solidarity ("The Leaning City"), muse ("Ruth, Who Was a Lark"), lover ("Beautiful Words," "The Swan," "Sea in the Air"), absolute companion ("I Will Bear You on My Brow," "Simple," "The Station and the Pact"), woman is all of these and more, a person in her own right who is consubstantial to the poet's own being. Woman has seldom been so fully realized in poetry.

The four decades of Sosa's career have been dark and dangerous times in Central America. To earn a precarious living, he has variously sold bread, measured heights, worked as a newspaperman and taught classes. But to survive—personally, ethically, as a human being of compassion and integrity—he depends entirely on poetry. "Poetry," he wrote recently, "is the last remaining lighthouse in the universe." Few poets have tended the light so faithfully.

Jo Anne Engelbert

EL LLANTO DE LAS COSAS
THE WEEPING OF THINGS

I

El Llanto de las Cosas

The Weeping of Things

Recuerdos número 1 - 2

A Roberto Armijo y Alfonso Quijada Urías

Mi primer recuerdo
parte de un farol a oscuras y se detiene
frente a un grifo público goteando hacia el interior de una calleja muerta.

Mi segundo recuerdo
lo desborda un muerto,
una procesión de muertos violentamente muertos.

Memories Numbers 1 - 2

To Roberto Armijo and Alfonso Quijada Urías

My earliest memory
starts at a burnt-out streetlight
and ends at a public spigot dripping
in a dead alley.

My second memory trickles from a corpse
a procession of corpses violently dead.

El pequeñín

A Juan Ramón Molina

Una y otra vez el pequeñín acertaba a decir a los que viajaban en aquel tren de carga—por piedad señores páguenme el pan que me han quitado, por piedad—y aquellos seres, dotados con formas humanas y sangre de gallo hasta el nivel del iris, flotaban a los lados y reían para adentro. Llovía a cántaros, con odio, rencorosamente llovía. El silbido del tren de carga era alto una y otra vez.

The Child

A Juan Ramón Molina

Again and again he managed to say to the men in the freight car, "Please misters, pay me for the bread you took, please," and those beings endowed with human form and rooster blood up to their pupils bobbed around him shaking with silent laughter. The rain fell hard, in vicious, spiteful torrents. The train blared its whistle again and again.

El llanto de las cosas

Mamá
se pasó la mayor parte de su existencia
parada en un ladrillo, hecha un nudo,
imaginando
que entraba y salía
por la puerta blanca de una casita
protegida
por la fraternidad de los animales domésticos.
Pensando
que sus hijos somos
lo que quisimos y no pudimos ser.
Creyendo
que su padre, el carnicero de los ojos gateados
y labios delgados de juez severo, no la golpeó
hasta sacarle sangre, y que su madre, en fin,
le puso con amor, alguna vez, la mano en la cabeza.
Y en su punto supremo, a contragolpe, como desde un espejo,
rogaba a Dios
para que nuestros enemigos cayeran como gallos apestados.

De golpe, una por una, aquellas amadísimas imágenes
fueron barridas por hombres sin honor.

Viéndolo bien
todo esto lo entendió esa mujer apartada,
ella
la heredera del viento, a una vela. La que adivinaba
el pensamiento, presentía la frialdad
de las culebras
y hablaba con las rosas, ella, delicado equilibrio
entre
la humana dureza y el llanto de las cosas.

The Weeping of Things

Mama
spent most of her life
standing on a brick, her body in a knot,
imagining she was going in and out of the white door
of a little house
protected by the brotherhood of domestic animals.
Thinking
her children were
what we tried to be
instead of what we were.
Believing
her father, the butcher with gold cat-eyes
and the thin lips of a judge,
did not beat her
till she bled, and that one day her mother
laid a loving hand on her brow.
From the apex of her thought, obliquely, as if
from the far side of a mirror,
she would pray God
that our enemies be struck down like sickly fowl.

Abruptly all the images she loved
were swept away by despicable men.

In time
this too was understood
by that lonely woman
to whom the wind
bequeathed a candle. She who read our thoughts,
sensed by their chill the proximity of snakes
and talked to roses, she, delicate balance
between
human hardness and the weeping of things.

Cansancio

A Rigoberto Paredes

No conozco la nieve.
Quizá el cansancio no sea sino la sensación de nieve de un balazo
en el cielo de la boca.

El patio viene a mí al son alegre de una media muerte y me habla
de mi pueblo y su fiesta tristísima,
del caballito que se quedó dormido en el cuaderno de dibujo
y de las señales que nos hizo la felicidad a todos y a cada uno
aquel día estrellado;
de papá y mamá me habla el patio inaccesible como un niño.

La media luz se ha vuelto áspera hasta el sonido rojo.

Oigo
las voces quebradas de mi gente
que tienen
la forma remota
de un adiós.

Weariness

To Rigoberto Paredes

I don't know snow.
Perhaps weariness is simply snow
snow chill
of a bullet through the roof of the mouth.

At the glad sound of a half death the patio comes to me
talking about the town
its sad fiestas,
the little horse asleep in the drawing pad
and the joy that waved to each and every one of us
on that star-shattered day;
about mama and papa too
that patio rambles on, inaccessible as a child.

The twilight has grown harsh since the red sound.

I hear
the broken voices of my people
mouthing
the distant shape
of a goodbye.

Los sucesos de aquel puerto

To Giovanni Papini

Su padre la llevaba en hombros y un jovencillo en lágrimas partido, delante, izaba una palma blanquísima bajo aquella tormenta cerrada. (La multitud armada de cirios idénticos avanzaba y retrocedía en orden perfecto, demasiado perfecto, y allá arriba, alrededor de un cono truncado giraba un pez brillante mordiéndose la cola: El Infinito.)

A imitación de la caída sensual de la melancolía del pantano el padre echó la última paletada de tierra sobre el cuerpecito de su hija Cristina alcanzando a graves penas a decir Dios no existe, y, camino a casa y solo como el espacio para él murió su flor, como si el jovencillo literalmente hablando, no hubiera podido despertarse un año antes de los sucesos de aquel puerto.

The Events in That Port

To Giovanni Papini

Her father carried her on his shoulders and up ahead a thin boy torn by tears lifted a pure white palm to the driving rain. (The multitude, armed with identical candles, advanced and retreated in perfect order, too perfect, and on high around a truncated cone spun a brilliant fish biting his tail: Infinity.)

With the voluptuous slowness of the gloom settling down upon the marsh, the father sifted the last spadeful of earth over his Cristina's small body, barely finding the breath to utter God does not exist, and on the way home, lonelier than space, he felt his flower die, as if that thin boy had literally been unable to awaken a whole year before the events in that port.

Lo cubra el mar lo cubra

Ha muerto.
Ernesto Mejía Sánchez
ha muerto.
Hizo de la sonrisa su recuerdo perfecto.

Dueño era del caballo vertical de la poesía y a fe de bueno
alzaba
en plena cara de los impostores el argumento fino
de su bastón de ciego.

Amó su Nicaragua como a nadie
y sentado está
a la izquierda
de Rubén Darío, fuera del maleficio.

Lo cubra el mar lo cubra.

Let the Sea Cover Him Let It Cover Him

He has died.
Ernesto Mejía Sánchez
has died.
He made a smile his perfect souvenir.
Master
of the vertical horse of poetry
he faithfully shook
in the faces of tongue-darting impostors
his blindman's cane.

He loved no one
more than he loved his Nicaragua
and he shall sit
at the left hand of Rubén Darío, free of the spell.

Let the sea cover him let it cover him.

Esa parte otra del misterio de la vida

Entonces no es mentira: nuestro hermano mayor se nos ha ido.

Por qué precisamente a Andrés Morris le tocó esa parte otra
                    del misterio de la vida,
y por qué, pregunto, no le tocó, por ejemplo
al más poderoso de los canallas de este planeta con todo
                    y su banquete de serpientes.

No.
No es verdad que haya muerto si ayer mismo una loca adorable
en plena calle le besó la frente. No puede ser, caramba.
Lo que pasa es que Andrés, a su estilo y medida, ha retornado
a su casita de Tegucigalpa y ha recobrado su segundo pueblo
como él quiso. Eso es todo.

Ahora está escribiendo su escritura, salvándose y sangrando.
Se oye irresistible el zumbido azul de una mosca
en la estancia.

Fuma y tose.
Busca la dulzura del barman o ríe de puro niño del cascabel del gato.
Maldice y resplandece.

Como si nada hubiera sucedido
de espaldas al olvido camina sobre el Tiempo...paso a paso
seguido por Guaribi, su perro llorón.

New York, NY, 12 de diciembre de 1987

That Other Part of the Mystery of Life

Then it's no lie: our big brother's gone away for good.

Why does it have to be Andrés Morris who begins that other part
of the mystery of life,
and why, I ask, not someone else, for instance
the planet's most powerful bully
and his banquet of vipers?

No.
He can't be dead if only yesterday an adorable crazy woman
stopped him on the street and kissed his brow. Christ, it can't be true.
It's just one of his tricks. Andrés has taken it into his head
to come back to his Tegucigalpa home and claim his second clan
as he always said he would. That's all.

He's writing a piece right now, saving his soul and bleeding.
The irresistible buzzing of a fly can be heard
in the room.

He smokes and coughs.
He looks around for a barman's sweet grin
or laughs like a child at the cat's little bell.
He swears and gives off light.

As if nothing had happened
with his back to oblivion he walks out onto Time... step by step
his pup Guaribi whimpering at his heels.

New York, NY, December 12, 1987

Del odio

A Inés Consuelo Murillo

Flotaba como una ola encrespándose la hermosísima mata de pelo
a cada impacto.

Intensos y pálidos
y creyendo como creen los idiotas del odio
que puede hacerse añicos la belleza, la hicieron picadillo.

Se equivocaron, claro, en el menor desvío de su línea recta
porque
fusil en mano ha vuelto la muchacha guerrillera: mirenlá.

On Hate

To Inés Consuelo Murillo

Her beautiful mass of hair floated like a wave, bristling
at each impact.

Intense and pale
and believing as the fools of hate believe
that beauty can be shattered like a flask
they drilled her into meat.

They erred, of course, by the slightest deflection from their straight line
because, look,
over there, her rifle in her hand, the guerrilla
reappears.

El viejo Pontiac

A Diana y Leonor

A la altura de su propia medida el viejo Pontiac es un jardín
que se abre.

Antes,
de esto hace ya muchísimo,
fingía un tigre manso deslizándose blanco entre mujeres bellas.

Hoy por hoy
el noble bruto envejece dignamente y sin prisa
hasta la consumación de los siglos... y le salen
de puertas y ventanas
florecillas del campo.

The Old Pontiac

To Diana and Leonor

In the fullness of its days the old Pontiac is a garden in bloom.

Once,
a lifetime ago,
it pretended to be a tiger gliding white among lovely women.

Today
the noble brute is aging gracefully and without haste
toward the consummation of the centuries...and growing out
of its doors and windows
are sprays of small white flowers.

Llama del bosque

A Ricardo Huerta

Allí esperó inclinado el caballito dos días incontables una señal de vida de su mama después del empujón terrible, fijos los ojos ya en el techo del mundo. Iba y venía esa clase de gente que poco o nada entiende de las cosas propias de los caballos en paso de peligro. Estuvo, así niñino, desnudo de dolor por dentro junto a su yegua blanca sosteniendo, intacto como la llama del bosque, la más hermosa lección de solidaridad dada entre el reino animal, en espera conmigo, de que la madre muerta de pronto describiera el signo del llamado del corazón del monte, tonto de él y tonto de mí, caballos.

Flame Tree

To Ricardo Huerta

For two uncountable days after the terrible crush the little horse looked down waiting for a sign of life from his mother, whose eyes were now fixed on the dome of heaven. The kinds of people passing by cared little or nothing about the ways of horses in the path of danger. Small and naked in his pain, he kept vigil beside his white mare, constant as a flame tree, a perfect lesson in animal solidarity. Side by side we waited for his mother to answer the call from the heart of the wild. Foolish of him, of me, horses.

Los pesares juntos

Aquí
hijas del verbo: madres, los esperaremos.

Escúchennos, "vivos se los llevaron, vivos los queremos."
Recuérdenlo en el nombre del padre, del hijo y del hermano
detenidos y desaparecidos.

Esperaremos con la frente en alto
punto por punto unidas como la cicatriz a sus costuras.

Nadie podrá destruir ni desarmar nuestros pesares juntos.
Amén.

The Common Grief

We
daughters and mothers of the word
wait for them
here.

Hear us. "Alive they took them, alive we want them back."
Heed us, in the name of the father and the son and the brother
detained and disappeared.

We wait with heads unbowed
fused stitch by stitch like a scab to the sutures of a wound.

No one can sever or divide our common grief.
Amen.

II

Historia Universal

Universal History

La casa donde habita la poesía

A Julio Andrade Yacamán y Carlos Villar Rosales

El ave fénix, única y verdadera, es la poesía.
Si pudiéramos mirarla siquiera,
dijimos.

Por ese camino y amados por el fuego
llegamos
a los pies de la gente de pueblo, y ahí,
fuera de nuestros límites
pudimos ver a ras de suelo y pobre como una estrella
la casa donde habita la poesía.

The House Where Poetry Lives

To Julio Andrade Yacamán and Carlos Villar Rosales

If we could only see her,
we said,
the only real phoenix,
poetry.

Bent to that road and loved by fire,
we came at last
to the feet of the people. There,
just out of reach
we saw
level with the ground and poor as a star
the house where poetry lives.

Historia universal

A Nelson E. Merren

Vamos a ver, dijo Borges, y en la eternidad quedó.

Universal History

To Nelson E. Merren

Borges said,"Let's see," and flipped

into eternity.

Una gaviota

A Jo Anne Engelbert

Todo
ha quedado a nivel y escuadra
detrás
de la serenidad de una cortina de cristal a prueba de golpes.
Todo.

No existe en Nueva York el paraguas para un corazón bajo la lluvia.

La multitud, observen, cubre con una sábana de hielo la rubia
hecha pedazos quién sabe por quién, ignora pan en mano, o no
puede moverse paralizada por un solo de violín
ejecutado
en el noveno círculo de la Gran Manzana.

(Pasa una mujer bella como ella sola y uno
desea ser su reloj de pulsera, su memoria de gringa de agua dulce,
su cinturón y el brazo que la ciñen
negros
como los extremos del mar océano.)

Fríos y distantes caballeros y damas de pupilas doradas
por el fulgor del dólar ¿qué hicieron del amor qué hicieron? Por
el bebé atrapado en un derrumbe, respondan. Esa es la pregunta.

Miren, Whitman y Poe tristemente regresan del futuro.
Miren allá miren, de la urbe y su animal impaciente
al que nadie pudo
verle dos veces los dientes, queda en pie un muñeco de nieve
en cuyo hombro derecho duerme una gaviota, testigo único
de lo irrepetible.

Corre el año 2030 del día 18 d abril de la Era Cristiana,
después de Einstein.

A Seagull

To Jo Anne Engelbert

Everything is squared off with a rule
behind the calm
of a plate of fistproof glass.
Everything.

New York has no umbrella for a heart pelted by rain.

Look, the crowd lays a sheet of ice over that blonde
hacked up by God knows who,
look at them, numb to it all, stopping to gawk
at a violin solo
played in the ninth circle of the Big Apple.

(A woman beautiful as only she herself passes by and goes
around a corner
and I
would like to be her wristwatch, her mind's eye—
                                    that of a blue-eyed latina—
or her belt and the arm around her waist,
both black
as the rim of the ocean sea.)

Cold and distant ladies and gentlemen, pupils gilded
by the dollar's glow, what have you done to love, what have you done?
In the name of the infant trapped in rubble, answer. That is the question.

Look at Whitman and Poe returning sadly from the future.
Look over there, look—of this whole city and its snapping animal
whose teeth no one has seen a second time
the only thing left standing is a snowman
on whose right shoulder dozes a seagull, sole witness to the unrepeatable.

It is now
the year 2030, 18th day of April of the Christian Era after Einstein.

La Ceiba

A Hernán Antonio Bermúdez

Ciudad, muy buenos días—¿sigues siendo la de antes?

Mi colegial cabeza
con los ojos de ciervo degollado—¿la recuerdas?

¿Quién domestica el mar al rojo vivo?

Mis amigos de entonces: Boris, Roland,
Alina la suave y el patio del silencio—¿dónde fueron?

Y Spilsbury,
el hombre aquel del manotazo negro—¿qué se hizo?—

Entre ese tiempo y éste he llegado a saber que yo soy
nadie
igual que una bahía.

Hoy apenas te veo. Traigo arena en los ojos y
la ilusión callada.
Fuiste la sola que no me hizo daño y para ti este canto,
ciudad buena.

1960-1989

44

La Ceiba

To Hernán Antonio Bermúdez

Good morning, city. Are you the same old place?

My schoolboy head, do you remember it, all eyes,
like a decapitated fawn?

Who tames your red hot sea these days?

My old friends, Boris, Ronald,
that sweet Alina and the silent patio—where are they now?

And Spilsbury, the guy with that awful black wallop,
whatever happened to him?

Between then and now I only learned one thing: I'm
nobody
just like the bay.
I can't see you too well today. I've got sand in my eyes, my illusions
are going dim.
You're the only one who never let me down, good city,
here's a poem for you.

1960-1989

III

La Puerta Unica

The Only Door

El tiempo

A Eduardo Bähr y Víctor Meza

La vida pasa y suelta su manzana podrida.

El Tiempo gira y cambia la creación entera: la bestia
se hará espuma: derivarán entonces
en jardines de niños las prisiones,
el oro, su infinito, o el odio del hombre por el hombre,
al fin de su jornada será una pajarita de papel.

Nuestro gran día mientras no amanece.

La existencia, la nuestra, es la de aquéllos
que tienen las manos metidas en el fuego y el Tiempo
semeja
un nudo corredizo alrededor del cuello.

Los árboles estallan en lágrimas por sus hermanos árboles.

Yo paso. Y usted pasa,
en tanto.

Time

To Eduardo Bähr and Víctor Meza

Life moves on and drops its rotten apple.

Time turns and all creation changes. Beasts
will turn to foam and jails to kindergartens.
Gold, its infinity, or the hate of man for man
will be by the end of this affair
mere paper birds.

Meanwhile our great day doesn't dawn.

We live like those
whose hands are in the fire
who know Time
as a noose around the neck.

Trees burst into tears for fellow trees.

I'm moving on. Before long
so will you.

Patria mía

A Ramón Oquelí

Hablando solo
del significado de los guardaespaldas de la Muerte,
pidiendo pan al hambre y cobija al frío,
así paso,
sintiendo la desolación de la desolación.

Abatido en la práctica por el fuego cruzado
que procede
de las palabras sueltas en labios de gente deshabitada para siempre,
caigo
como una piedra lanzada desde la hondonada del cielo.

Llevado y traído
por el desorden del mar de papeles sucios que ello supone,
así he vivido mi vida, traicionado a fondo,
buscando
el espacio más limpio de la página en blanco
que me permita, al fin, sin avergonzarme ya, escribir tu nombre,
patria mía.

Dear Country

To Ramón Oquelí

Muttering to myself
about the meaning of the bodyguards of Death,
asking hunger for bread, the tempest for a roof,
I get by,
knowing the despair of despair.

Cut down in action by the crossfire
of stray words on the lips of long-vacated people,
I fall
like a stone flung from the bowels of heaven,
a bullet in my wing.

Heaved about
by the sea of filthy papers spewing up,
betrayed to the bone,
I've spent my life
looking for one clean spot
where at last,
dear country,
I could write your name
unashamed.

Siempre Honduras siempre

A Ezequiel Padilla Ayestas, Aníbal Cruz y Obed Valladares

Noche y día
propios y extraños repiten sin descanso: éste
no es un país, es un paisaje y se hunde definitivamente.
Y agregan
como los que creen haber salido
del final de un laberinto ¿cómo pueden quererlo así?
Por eso mismo, les decimos nosotros, porque es un país niño,
tanto que todavía el pobre ni siquiera ha aprendido
a llover.

Honduras Forever and Ever

To Ezequiel Padilla Ayestas, Aníbal Cruz and Obed Valladares

Hondurans, non-Hondurans, everyone keeps up the chant:
"It's a landscape, not a land... and it's damned."

And they add
with a knowing air
as if they had just found their way out of a maze,
who could love such a runt of a place?

And we say, that's why we love it... It's such a little country—
the poor thing hasn't even learned
how to rain.

Los brutales amantes

A Filánder Díaz Chávez y Adán Castelar

Ellos, los extraños,
llegaron de otros mundos a este suelo que nos vio nacer.
Somos la luz dijeron sin bosticar palabra.

Llegaron
multiplicando muertes por traiciones a llamarnos amigos,
a comérselo todo y a quedarse en este suelo
que nos vio nacer, ellos los hombres lineales y metálicos,
ellos,
los brutales amantes de la Muerte.

Muerte a la Muerte.

The Brutal Lovers

To Filánder Díaz Chávez and Adán Castelar

They, the aliens,
came from other worlds
to this land that saw our birth.
We are the light, they said, not mincing words.

They arrived,
multiplying deaths by treachery,
called us their friends,
sucked up all we had and made themselves at home
in this land that saw our birth,
they, the linear and metallic ones,
they,
the brazen lovers of Death.

Death to Death.

La eternidad y un día

A Francisco Salvador

Se hace tarde, cada vez más tarde.
Ni el viento pasa por aquí y hasta la Muerte es parte
del paisaje.

Bajo su estrella fija Tegucigalpa es una ratonera.

Llorar por todos
quiero.
Matar podría ahora y en la hora en que ruedan sin amor las palabras.

Solo el dolor llamea
en este instante que dura ya la eternidad
y un día.

¿Qué hacer?
¿Qué hacer?

Alguien que siente y sabe de qué habla
exclama, por mejor decir, musita:—hagamos algo pronto,
hermanos míos, por favor, muy pronto.

Eternity and a Day

To Francisco Salvador

It's getting late, later and later.
The wind won't blow here any more and Death is now a part
of the terrain.

Under its fixed star Tegucigalpa is a knot of mice.

I want to weep
for everyone.
I could kill, now and in the hour of words uttered without love.

Nothing flickers now but pain
in this instant that is already eternity
and a day.

What can we do?
What can we do?

Someone who cares and knows what she is saying
exclaims, or rather, whispers: "We must act soon,
my brothers, please, it must be soon."

La puerta única

A Juan Octavio Valencia

En alguna parte, en estos momentos,
alguien
confusamente complacido escribe en pulcro idioma
la ciencia de la mentira.

Entretanto sobre numerosos puntos de nuestro planeta
grupos de exniños
deslumbrados por el éxtasis del cierre de caja
agonizan de hambre.

Sin embargo, cerca o lejos,
existen otros seres humanos que creen en el derecho a la belleza
y aceptan
que esta mañana refleja la puerta única
por donde se puede entrar a la felicidad a título de pueblo
liberado.

Tegucigalpa, 1969-1987

The Only Door

To Juan Octavio Valencia

Somewhere at this very moment
someone
in confused complacency
is setting down in beautiful language
the science of lying.

Meanwhile, at different points on our planet,
groups of ex-children
dazzled by the gleam of cash registers
writhe in hunger.

Nevertheless, far or near,
there are other human beings who believe in the right to beauty,
who understand
that this morning is the only door
through which we can enter happiness
as a liberated people.

Tegucigalpa, 1969-1987

Bajo un árbol

A Ramón Custodio

Este hombre sin pan, ese sin luces y aquel sin voz
equivalen al cuerpo de la patria,
a la herida y su sangre abotonada.

Contemplen el despojo:
nada nos pertenece y hasta nuestro pasado se llevaron.

Pero aquí viviremos.

Con la linterna mágica del hijo que no ha vuelto
abriremos de par en par la noche.
De la nostalgia por lo que perdimos
iremos construyendo un sueño a piedra y lodo.

Guardamos, los vencidos, ese sabor del polvo que mordimos.

Junto a esto
que a veces es algo menos que triste,
bajo un árbol,
desnudos si es preciso, moriremos.

Under a Tree

To Ramón Custodio

This man without bread, this child without light and
                                        that woman without a voice
equal this country's body,
its wound and its coagulated blood.

The pillage is complete.
We've nothing to our name: they even stole our past.

But we will go on living here.

With the magic lantern of the son who disappeared
we will open wide the night.
Of mud, of stone,
of grief for what we lost,
we'll make a dream.

We who were conquered remember the taste of the dust we had to bite.

And in this place
which is sometimes less than sad,
under a tree,
naked if need be, we'll die.

MÁSCARA SUELTA
THE LIFTED MASK

I

Máscara Suelta
The Lifted Mask

La desconocida

Las tres bellas mujeres idénticas
son y han sido en estricta verdad
una sola: la mujer
que lucha con la sombra del fuego
del hogar
es igual al más bello animal de la Tierra,
igual a su vez
a la oficiante alta y delgada que noche tras noche
sobreviene durante el sueño hasta el sol de
hoy.

She

In strict truth
the three identical
beautiful women
are and always have been
one. The woman who wrestles with the shadow
of the hearth
is the same as the most beautiful animal on Earth,
who in turn is the same
as the tall priestess
who night after night
has ravished me in dreams
until the dawning of
this day.

El mar en el aire

A pie, sin volver la mirada,
recorro el despiadado sendero.

Percibo claramente
el ascenso y descenso de tu respiración.

Te acercas y te alejas
detrás
de tu invertida sonrisa inexplicable.

Acaso el confín
que conduce contra el reloj su automóvil de antiquísimo modelo
observa
la marcha sufridora.

Siento el verano que baja tortuoso por tus venas y justo
en el cruce de tu vientre la hebra de oro en ascuas
que hace a tu cuerpo abrirse como un libro de páginas en blanco.

De la sucesión de ese espacio-tiempo de la melancolía cálida
de tu semblante depende la prolongación de la hora que vivo.

¿Qué temblor no he partido? Y el sendero no acaba y me lastima
segundo tras segundo.

Tegucigalpa, 1982

Sea in the Air

On foot, without a backward glance
I trudge the brutal path

rapt
in the ebb and flow
of your breath.

Behind
an unexplainable inverted smile
you wax and wane.

Does the horizon
driving its ancient car against the clock
observe my faltering?

I see summer gliding down your veins
to the strand of incandescent gold
at the cross
of your umbilicus.
Your body opens like a book
of unwritten pages.

On the time space shimmer of your melancholy gaze
depends
the prolongation of this hour of my life.

How many earthquakes have I crumbled? The path
winds on forever,
wounding me.

Tegucigalpa, 1982

La muerte enamorada

El agua enamorada te descubre
conmigo. Como lo sabe hacer se disminuye a tu proximidad
y cuida tu vestido amarillo tirado en la playa y malherido,
aún tibio.

De pie, como la hermosa desconocida, la Muerte
mortalmente enamorada.

Inadvertidamente coge un pájaro y dilátanle las plumas sus pupilas.
La eternidad del pájaro perdura en el impulso
de su propia medida: quema cantando su licor milenario
y no sabe ni trata de entenderlo, es parte
de la fragilidad de lo que está perfecto.

La admiramos sin mirarla.

La más puntual de las amantes cruza, profesional,
la estancia sin mirarnos y nos ha permitido, por lo mismo,
sobrevivir lo indispensable para poder volver a sentir
el temblor que te produce lo que callo
en estas palabras.

Tegucigalpa, 1982

Amorous Death

The enamored water surprises you with me.
It shrinks from you as it knows how and strokes
your crumpled yellow dress upon the shore, wounded
and still warm.

Death loiters
pale and beautiful
and pierced by love.

Absently, she plucks a bird from the air and its plumes dilate her
                                                                    pupils.
The bird's eternity persists in the impulse
of its form: it does not know nor try to understand.
It burns, singing its ancient liquor, part of the fragility
of perfection.

The stranger thrills us though we do not meet her gaze.

The most correct of lovers, she crosses the day
with a professional air, without looking at us, and allows us to survive
the indispensable instant to absorb
the throb I silence
in these words.

Tegucigalpa, 1982

La brevedad ilímite

Otro tiempo
nos contuvo abrazados como dos niños ciegos
a punto de caer en la noche de los objetos.

Mi frente tarde. Duro el azar supuesto.

Blanca y desnuda la selva no existía a tu lado.
Nada
había en el límite sino la marea en tus ojos.

Busqué tu afecto, su música de agua, con la intensidad
con que suelen hacerlo los sentenciados al sacrificio final,
flor arriba, dormido.

Entonces, cualquier cosa,
por ejemplo una pluma nos cubría la memoria de pájaros.

La brevedad ilímite del dolor de vivir
no era más que el instante de la estrella en el piso,
el reflejo del bosque en una hoja, o tal vez la nostalgia
del carruaje en su estacionamiento.

Boundless Brevity

A different time contained us
when we clung to one another
like two blind children about to fall
into the night of objects.

My aging brow. Harsh, our so called fate.

Beside your nakedness the jungle
vanished. Nothing
was.
To the far horizon, only the green sea
of the iris of your eyes.

I sought your love, its water music, with the fever
of one marked for sacrifice,
upflower, in a dream.

Then any little thing...
a feather for example filled our memory with birds.

The boundless brevity of the ache of life
was no more than a point of starlight on the ground,
the reflection of the forest on a leaf, or perhaps the yearning
of a carriage waiting at the gate.

La estación y el pacto

Ni la ventana que entredibuja el viejo campanario.
Ni aquella ingenuidad de primer grado
del insecto viudo que aún sobrevuela mi infancia.
Ni la amistad del libro: me hacen falta.

Tus manos al alcance de mis manos
me faltan
como las compartidas soledades.

Necesito, lo sabes, las gemelas alturas de tu cuerpo,
su blancura quemada. Y ese pez
que vuela azulinante hacia el final de tus desnudeces...
abriendo y cerrando los labios de tu fuerza oscurísima.

The Station and the Pact

Not my window framing a distant spire
nor the innocence of the widowed lightning bug
pulsing above the schoolyard of my youth.
Nor the fellowship of books: these
I do not need.

I need
your hands within the reach of my hands
as I need to share
my solitary days.

I need, and you know, the twin heights of your breasts,
their burned whiteness. And that fish
that leaps habluecinated to the farthest reaches of your nakedness...
opening and closing the lips
of your dark force.

El regreso del río

Ha regresado el río.

Paseamos, como antes, por lugares poblados
de ruidos del bosque y de nombres. Hablamos
de personas y sucesos que casi nadie sabe que trazaron mi rumbo.

Evocamos, estrechándonos más de lo necesario, la armonía
del valle atormentado que conduce
a espumosos países donde la mansedumbre cuida de la niñez.

(Se dibuja rojiza la caída del cisne
que en pleno vuelo se destrozó contra tu cabellera.)

Ha regresado el río a su vuelta primera
y ha hecho
que tu presencia persista en eso que ha quedado de la música.

The Return of the River

The river has returned.

We walk, as before, through places echoing
with forest sounds and names. We talk
of friends and little known events
that shaped my course.

Half embracing we evoke the harmony
of the tormented valley that leads to airy lands
where kindness minds the young.

(A red line marks the falling of the swan
that perished in the glory of your hair.)

The river has returned to its first curve
but you linger
in these shards of music that remain.

La fuente iluminada

Digo mar y te identifico y me pregunto
qué principio desborda el vaso que te vuelve fraterna
y de dónde procede el flujo y reflujo del agua lejanísima
que hace a tus senos subir y bajar su hermosura.

Desde mi cama puedo tocar las ramas y piedras
que labra la paciencia marina y de este modo enciendo
un rayo de sol del mundo comprendido
que ha de sobrevivirnos.

Digo mar, y olvido, un instante,
los agujeros de aquellas máscaras envejecidas por el odio
desde
donde
me observa cierta gente que trato día a día.

The Illuminated Fountain

I say sea and name you
and wonder what potion overbrimming the glass
has made you kin
what flux and reflux of distant water
makes your breasts lift
and lower their beauty.

From my bed I touch the twigs and stones
the patient sea is carving. I cast a ray of sun
into the world that will survive us.

I say sea and forget, for an instant,
the holes in hate-wizened masks through which certain people
peer at me each day.

Ciudad inclinada

La tierra firme te hizo melancólica.

Fraterna te he llamado
porque sufres notables alteraciones anímicas,
sobre todo al filo de la aparición de los primeros luceros
de tus estados crepusculares,
ante
los rosados arañazos
causados
por las ráfagas de tos que sacuden
a determinados vecindarios, aquellos, bien lo sabes,
para quienes ese cielo que vemos
limpio hasta la pared de enfrente
es brusco en su caída dentro de los espacios alambrados.

Allí, demasiado próxima a los más bajos niveles
de humanas figuras y planos descendidos a pausas,
has contemplado al pie de un firmamento empedrado
                                        la ciudad inclinada,
decir quiero
la infancia acorralada por perros de sombras amaestradas
con sangrientos sonidos o el espanto de la belleza
con un pie atrapado en una curva de la línea férrea.

Y allí, a pesar de tu amor
por los autobuses que corren hacia las orillas del mundo
entre los gritos de la llanura apagándose en circunferencias,
y a pesar de tu amor
por los ciervos que pacen sobre el césped de la Biblia
y por el universo en expansión, el otro, que soñó el viejo Marx,
tu verdadera imagen ha sido negada con palabras audaces.

Allí mismo me he emocionado y he dejado al lado de rendijas y goteras
lo que queda de mi duración.

Leaning City

Terra firma made you melancholy.

I called you kin
because even with the first stars of your twilight
your mood changed
if you heard the pink scratching, gusts of coughing
that rattle certain neighborhoods
where the sky we see clear to the horizon
falls brusquely into barbed-wire lots.

There, too close to the lowest rung of life
of human shapes and planes shrunken to pauses,
you stood at the foot of a stony sky and viewed
the leaning city,
I mean
childhood cornered by mastiffs with trained shadows,
blighted by bloody sounds or a fear of beauty,
a foot trapped in a curve of the railroad track.

And there, despite your love
of buses that run to the rim of the world
over shouting plains that hush near the circumference,
and despite your love for the deer that graze on the lawn of the Bible
and for the expanding universe, the one Old Marx dreamed of,
your true face was erased
by arrogant words.

And in that place I wept and left among the leaks and cracks
the little that remains of my duration.

De la bruma hice vino

Amiga mía, bella
como la mujer bellísima que cruzó hacia la locura,
no hubo signo en mi origen que no te enamorara.

¿Qué complicados golpes no convertí en azúcar?

De la bruma hice vino, del vino sangre,
de la sangre, sobre el primer nivel de mi elección,
hice el dibujo perfecto de tus labios.

Jamás dijiste algo
que ofendiera la dignidad pacífica de las cosas del campo.

Indestructible y tierna te elogiaron las piedras,
tu mirada elogiaron, limpia como un desierto.

Los hombres de este pueblón sin música no olvidarán
tu nombre.

From the Mist I Made Wine

Beloved, beautiful
as the most beautiful woman who crossed over into madness,
there was no sign in my beginning but led me to love you.

What complicated blows did I not convert to sugar?

From the mist I made wine, from the wine I made blood,
from blood beyond the reach of my desire
I made a perfect picture of your lips.

You have never said a word that might disturb
the peaceful dignity of country things.

The stones have praised you, indestructible and tender,
they have praised your clear gaze,
open as the desert.

The people of this poor town without music
will not forget your name.

Así de sencillo

Para Lidia

Mujer, la de la mano amiga sobre el hombro,
los extremos se tocan, con amor, en tus dedos.

Juntos
recorreremos el andado y desandado camino. Y nada
haremos que no sea hermoso.

Entre la oscura oscuridad oscura de los enamorados,
a riesgo de que pueda quebrarse
la unidad que sostiene tu cerrada belleza de niña pobre,
haremos huesos viejos.

Así de sencillo.

Simple

To Lidia

Wife, you of the gentle hand on my shoulder,
all extremes meet, with love, in your fingertips.

Together
we'll walk the traveled and retraveled roads. And nothing we do
will not be beautiful.

In the darkest dark darkness of lovers,
risking the unity that sustains your fragile grace—
shy beauty of a country girl—
we'll let our bones grow old.

Simple.

Vía muerta

Adiós, dijo. Y cerró la ciudad.

Ayer mismo, por su extrema ausencia,
la muñeca de barro, mi amiguita,
sin previo aviso se lanzó al vacío.
La biblioteca se deshoja. Los cuadros
se reducen a unas simples manchas.

Oigo por todas partes el grillo de la Luna.

Desciendo, el corazón en la mano, por la vía muerta
de un mal sueño del que ya no es posible despertar.

Dead End

Goodbye, she said. And closed the city.

Just yesterday, because of her extreme absence,
the clay doll, my little friend,
cast herself into the void.
The library has shed its leaves. Pictures blur
to shapeless stains.

The cricket of the Moon chirps endlessly.

With my heart in my hand I walk down a dead end street
in a dream from which I can't awaken.

Máscara suelta

Oye mi voz,
oye mi voz
porque antes
de que los reptiles se devoren entre sí
te llamarán con nombres alcanzados por el prestigio
del brillo del oro.

-Desnuda la mujer, te dirán con los ojos,
es un ángel de pie sobre la Tierra.

A cambio de lo que más adoras
te ofrecerán
la seguridad
de sus palacios que tienen la apariencia del aire,
sus vinos y sus rosas y sus inclinaciones, los manuscritos
que guardan sus llagas sagradas.

Oye mi voz, mi único amor, oye mi voz porque escrito está
que detrás de ese concéntrico espejismo se levantan de pronto
sus panteones, la prosa tísica, sus burdeles de oro,
la nieve negra y sus salpicaduras, la advertencia más seria
de la Muerte.

Tegucigalpa, 1987

The Lifted Mask

Heed my words,
beware:
before the vipers devour one another
they will call you with names bought with the prestige
of the gleam of gold.

"This woman disrobed," they will tell you with their eyes,
"is an angel
descended to the Earth."

In exhange for your honor
they will offer you the safety
of their palaces that look like air
their wines, their roses and their bows, the papers
that hide their holy sores.

Beware, my only love, for it is written
that their concentric mirages shall belch forth
whited sepulchers, golden brothels, unclean prose
and the black slush of their filth, the certain signs
of Death.

Tegucigalpa, 1987

II

El más Antiguo de los Nombres del Fuego

The Oldest of the Names of Fire

Ultimo verso de un epigrama

Toda mi vida amaría a María. Ah María, ah María.

Last Verse of an Epigram

All my life, Ah, Dora I adore. Ah!

La sal dulce de la palabra poesía

Del fuego, en un principio,
los dioses de los primeros hombres
que lo vieron y lo amaron fueron haciendo, solos,
la mujer.
Esculpieron temblando sus senos absolutos,
la ondulación del pelo,
la copa de su sexo, más complicada, por dentro,
que el interior de un caracol marino.

Delinearon a pulso la sombra de su sombra,
la curva y mordedura de ese juego del fuego
que sabe a rojo virgen debajo de la lengua
y levanta
la súbita belleza de una brasa en los ojos.

Desde entonces, su cuerpo
se hizo pudor tocable en carne y hueso.

Digo mujer,
la sal dulce de la palabra poesía.

Tegucigalpa, 1987

The Sweet Salt of the Word Poetry

Out of fire
the gods of the first men to see it and adore it
molded woman.

The sculpted her absolute breasts,
the undulation of her hair,
the chalice of her sex, more intricate within
than the recesses of a chambered shell.
They traced freehand the shadow of her shadow,
the leap and bite of fire's desire
that tastes virgin red beneath the tongue
and brings
the sudden beauty of an ember to the eye.

Since then
her body has become
the shyness
of pure naked skin
remote and touchable.

I say woman
sweet salt of the word poetry.

Tegucigalpa, 1987

Sobre el agua

Ella tiene los poderes del mar cintura adentro.

Una flor amarilla
su cabello disuelve en resplandores duros y pesados.

Desnuda así posee la atracción que siente la mariposa
seducida por la fuerza de la suavidad de la materia ávida y abierta.

Sus labios y palabras
acumulan la lengua de lo tibio y luchan entre sí hasta la muerte
antes
de convertirse en una melodía.

Más bella
la hace el dúctil y maleable mastín que la vigila.

Ella, confieso a medio arrullo,
está hecha de fuentes luminosas y su inteligencia es dulce
como el agua primera que dio origen al mundo.

Por ella, aquí, es menos doloroso el oficio de poeta.

Upon the Water

Her waist contains the powers of the sea.

Her hair
dissolves a yellow flower in molten splendors.

Naked like this she is the force that lures the moth to the softness
of avid yielding matter.

Her lips and words make a language of tenderness
that struggles to the death before becoming melody.

The sleek and supple mastiff standing guard
makes her more beautiful.

She, I confess half crooning,
is made of luminous fountains and her intelligence is pure
as the first water that gave birth to the world.

Because of her, it is less painful
to be a poet here.

Ruth, la que fue alondra

En el lugar que recuerda
la tierra de nadie, Ruth, la que fue alondra,
abría puntualmente
esa ventana que da al mar y una paloma blanca le sacaba
al espacio.

Bajo llave guardaba la tristeza.

Al filo de su tentación por la serenidad contemplaba
mis años como quien ve un abismo.

En silencio admiraba, y admira sin duda,
mi sentimentalismo tonto por las causas perdidas
y por la suerte de la última de las naciones.

Ella adoraba mi poesía y yo a ella y entré a su corazón
como un menor de edad
a su casa.

Ruth, Who Was a Lark

In a place that seemed like
no-man's-land, Ruth, who was a lark,
punctually raised
that window that opened on the sea
and released a dove.

She kept her sadness under lock and key.

From the pinnacle of her temptation to serenity
she looked upon my years as one looks into the void.

In silence she admired, and still admires, perhaps,
my fondness for lost causes
and for this, the least of nations.

She loved my poetry and I loved her and I entered her heart
like a child coming home.

Las hermosas palabras

Antes de aprender a escuchar el silencio y a descifrar
su música de cuerdas, sufrimos lo que no tiene nombre.

A la oración, a su caída en círculos, las hermosas palabras
te encendían el rostro.

Fascinados por la ley de los espejos descendimos
hasta la puerta del esplendor púrpura del centro de la cebolla,
y ahí, tendida y extendida,
pude en ese punto de la sangre dulce besar tu corazón.

Los cuerpos, a su placer, se anudaron y desanudaron
deslumbrados hasta bien entrada
la noche excesiva.

A nuestros pies estuvo la bóveda celeste.

Este cubo, su mar en miniatura, y estos objetos
pobres como las estrellas de mi República demuestran
que lo vivido por aquellos días
no fue un sueño.

Beautiful Words

Before we learned to listen to silence, to discern
its cello melodies, we suffered
the unnamable.

At Angelus beautiful words falling in spirals
made your face burn.

Dazzled by the law of mirrors we descended
to the door of purple splendor at the center of the onion,
and there, where you lay waiting,
I could kiss your heart
on that point
of sweet blood.

Our bodies twined and untwined at their pleasure
marveling
deep in the excessive night.

At our feet lay the celestial dome.

This cube, its miniature sea, and these objects,
poor as the stars of my Republic,
prove
that what we lived in those days
was not a dream.

El cisne negro

Tu nombre digo y beso tu blancura.

Tu nombre escribo y toco, hebra por hebra, el cisne negro del pubis.

El amor, el cuadro de su sombra,
es el músico cierre de una mano extendida a otra mano.

Una voz
dice tu nombre frente al mar y yo lo repito detrás del mar
y lo escribo en pedacitos de papel
que después esparzo bajo los puentes, para que nadie lo lea
ni lo toque.

The Black Swan

I speak your name and kiss your whiteness.

I write your name and touch, strand by strand, the black swan of
your pubis.

Love, its shadow on the screen,
is the melodic closing of a hand
that clasps another hand.

A voice speaks your name before the sea and I repeat it
where the sea can't hear
and I write it on bits of paper I scatter under bridges so that no one
can read it
or touch it.

Como un elogio

Día tras día por la tarde en punto recuerdo exactamente los grandes arcoiris cruzados a tu paso, los golpecillos clave, las cuatro o cinco frases llevadas en voz baja, los roces de los lados y el desplome sin ruido: hacia arriba tu ombligo como el centro perpetuo de la nieve.

Dentro de los espejos para siempre quedamos boca a boca enlazados, acaso entredormidos, fuera de las desgracias y los tiempos.

Han pasado muchísimas estrellas bajo los puentes de Tegucigalpa, ciudad condenada a ser bella. No me deja, mujer, tu singular manera de mirar a los ojos ni me suelta al crepúsculo la fuerza de tu efigie.

(La Mariposa Negra suspensa en el espacio o estática en el techo convoca sus poderes y despliega mezclados secretos y temores.)

No. No hay descanso posible debajo de la piel enamorada: caen los granos últimos de mi reloj de arena y mi sed no se apaga.

Allí donde la Tierra parece que se une con el cielo quedaron nuestros nombres como un elogio.

Tegucigalpa, 1987

A Kind of Praise

At twilight, I remember rainbows rising in your path, secret knocks, four or five hushed phrases, the graze of sides and a soundless falling, your navel perpetual center of the snows.

Even now we linger in those mirrors, mouth near mouth, drowsing perhaps, beyond time and care.

Many stars have passed beneath the bridges of Tegucigalpa, city destined to be be fair. Woman, your way of looking in my eyes still comforts me, and the virtue of your effigy protects me from the shade.

(The Black Butterfly quivers in air or poises on the ceiling, summoning its powers, unfurling random dread.)

No. Beneath enamored skin there is no peace: the last grains in my hourglass begin their slide and still, my burning thirst.

Along the line where Earth and heaven merge our names are written as a kind of praise.

Tegucigalpa, 1987

En este parque, solo

Así estabas: abandonada entre las propias cúspides doradas. Ajena a la mujer que se paseaba fuera de sí en la azotea aquella. Superior al hechizo del rostro sagrado del asesino profesional que miraba y admiraba tus muslos carceleros y el lirio de tus nalgas, inconcluso como un tigre enamorado. Tenías, a veces, el aire discreto y melancólico de la flor que suele haber en los hoteles.

De pie o acostada, desnuda o en traje blanco, la aguja flotante del miedo apuntaba insistente contra el sitio mástierno que divide tu cuerpo, y así, con los nervios de punta y unidos por un hilo irrompible oíamos murmullo por murmullo, allá a lo lejos al pie de un firmamento color azul teatro, el estruendo apagándose de una pelea a muerte.

En dónde estás, me digo, y qué haces con la media noche en torno a un vaso de vino y quién besa tu espalda como la magia, blanca.

Junto a esa estatua — mi amiga y tu doble — insisto como siempre con mi vieja pregunta: qué sería del frío de tu belleza si yo no lo acunara de tarde en tarde en este parque, solo.

Tegucigalpa, 1987

106

In This Park, Alone

Adrift among your own golden spires.A stranger to the frantic woman
prancing on the roof.Aloof to the spell of the angel-faced assassinpoised
like an amorous lynx before your subjugating thighsand the lily of your
buttocks.Sometimes you had the melancholy air of a floweron the desk
of a hotel.

Standing serenely or lying among pillows,nude or gowned in white, you
sensed the floatingneedle of fear pointing implacably to the tenderest
placethat divides your body. Against a firmament of theater blue,our
taut nerves linked by unbreakable wire, we listened murmur by murmur
to the distant sounds of a battle to the death.

Where are you now, I ask, and what will you do with this midnight
swirling about your wine glass, and who is kissing your shoulder, white
as magic.

Beside this statue—my companion and your double—I repeat my
ancient question: what would become of your beauty's coldness if I did
not come at dusk to cradle it in this park, alone.

Tegucigalpa, 1987

El más antiguo de los nombres del fuego

Dichosos los amantes porque les pertenece
el grano de arena
que sostiene el peso del centro de los mares.

Hipnotizados por los juegos de agua
no oyen
sino la música que sus nombres esparce.

Unidos,
pegándose entre sí como los animalitos aterrados
que presienten que van a morir, tiemblan sus partes.

Nada les es ajeno.

Para ellos contra viento y marea
sólo tienen sentido las embellecedoras palabras
de todo lo que existe:—te amo, juntos hacia el final
llegaremos a viejos.

Los cuervos y las cuervas les sacarán los ojos,
los bellos gestos, incluso la luna del espejo,
pero no el fuego,
de donde surgirán de nuevo los amantes.

The Most Ancient of the Names of Fire

Blessed are the lovers
for theirs is the grain of sand
that sustains the center of the seas.

Dazed by the play of fountains
they hear nothing
but the music sprinkled by their names.

Trembling
they cling to one another
like small frightened animals who tremble, knowing they will die.

Nothing is alien to them.

Their only strength against the wind and tide
are the beautifying words of all existence: I love you.
We shall grow old together to the end.

Male and female ravens steal lovers' eyes,
their beautiful gestures, even the moon in their mirror
but not the fire
from which they are reborn.

Curbstone Press, Inc.
is a non-profit publishing house dedicated to literature
that reflects a commitment to social change, with an emphasis
on contemporary writing from Latin America and Latino
communities in the United States. Curbstone presents writers
who give voice to the unheard in a language that goes beyond
denunciation to celebrate, honor and teach. Curbstone builds
bridges between its writers and the public – from inner-city to
rural areas, colleges to community centers, children to adults.
Curbstone seeks out the highest aesthetic expression of the
dedication to human rights and intercultural understanding:
poetry, testimonials, novels, stories, photography.

This requires more than just producing books.
It requires ensuring that as many people as possible know about
these books and read them. To achieve this, a large portion of
Curbstone's schedule is dedicated to arranging tours and
programs for its authors, working with public school and
university teachers to enrich curricula, reaching out to
underserved audiences by donating books and conducting
readings and community programs, and promoting discussion in
the media. It is only through these combined efforts that
literature can truly make a difference.

Curbstone Press, like all non-profit presses,
depends on the support of individuals, foundations,
and government agencies to bring you, the reader, works of
literary merit and social significance which might not find a place
in profit-driven publishing channels. Our sincere thanks to the
many individuals who support this endeavor and to the following
foundations and government agencies: ADCO Foundation,
J. Walton Bissell Foundation, Witter Bynner Foundation for
Poetry, Connecticut Commission on the Arts, Connecticut Arts
Endowment Fund, Lannan Foundation, LEF Foundation,
Lila Wallace-Reader's Digest Fund, Andrew W. Mellon
Foundation, National Endowment for the Arts
and The Plumsock Fund.

Please support Curbstone's efforts to
present the diverse voices and views that make our
culture richer. Tax-deductible donations can be made to
Curbstone Press, 321 Jackson Street, Willimantic, CT 06226